Stability and Differentiation in the European Union

T0098181

Stability and Differentiation in the European Union

Search for a Balance

Prof. Jaap W. de Zwaan

This publication is an elaborated version of the text of
the Farewell Lecture of Jaap de Zwaan as Professor European
Integration at the The Hague University of Applied Sciences,
delivered on 24 March 2017 and updated since

international publishing

Published, sold and distributed by Eleven International Publishing
P.O. Box 85576
2508 CG The Hague
The Netherlands
Tel.: +31 70 33 070 33
Fax: +31 70 33 070 30
e-mail: sales@elevenpub.nl
www.elevenpub.com

Sold and distributed in USA and Canada
International Specialized Book Services
920 NE 58th Avenue, Suite 300
Portland, OR 97213-3786, USA
Tel: 1-800-944-6190 (toll-free)
Fax: +1-503-280-8832
orders@isbs.com
www.isbs.com

Eleven International Publishing is an imprint of Boom uitgevers
Den Haag.

ISBN 978-94-6236-785-2
ISBN 978-94-6274-758-6 (E-book)

Printed in The Netherlands

TABLE OF CONTENTS

1 Introduction

The European Union (EU) cooperation is built upon principles such as unity and uniformity. These principles are fundamental assets to assure the stability of the overall EU institutional and legislative infrastructure.

These days, however, the European Union is faced with serious threats and challenges, both externally (tensions at the external EU borders, migration and terrorism) and internally (economic crisis, migration, populism and Brexit).

Practice shows that is it getting more and more difficult to arrive at timely and adequate common solutions to counter, *inter alia*, the threats and challenges mentioned. The reference in this context is notably to the differences of opinion between the present twenty-eight Member States as well as to the way competences and responsibilities are divided at present between the EU and its Member States.

Therefore, in order to ensure the continuation and further deepening of the integration process, the question arises whether structural formulas of differentiated cooperation should not be encouraged.

The central idea behind this approach basically is that it is better to facilitate those Member States who want to advance, instead of forcing the non-willing Member States to cooperate.

2 European Union

The European Union is a unique organisation. It is an international organisation which possesses its own competences, institutions, decision-making procedures, legal instruments, financial resources as well as legal personality. It is a framework enabling its Member States to closely cooperate – and integrate – in a variety of policy domains, such as the economy, monetary policy, justice and home affairs as well as foreign policy and defence. Strictly speaking there is hardly any policy domain where the Union is not entitled to act, if only in a coordinating manner.

Decision making essentially occurs at three levels. *Firstly*, the Member States, by concluding treaties and successive amending treaties, determine the scope of the objectives and substance matters to be dealt with by the EU, as well as the relevant decision-making procedures. *Secondly*, the European Council – the framework where Heads of State or Government do meet each other – determines and monitors the programming and timing of the activities of the EU. *Thirdly*, the institutions of the Union, according to an original set of procedures – referred to generally speaking as 'supranational' procedures – implement the treaty objectives, by making use of a specific set of legal instruments, and while taking into account the instructions adopted at the level of the European Council.

In the last context, the Commission has the power to present proposals, to be commonly decided upon by the Council of Ministers and the European Parliament. The Council – the representative body of the Member States – decides generally speaking by qualified majority whereas the directly elected European Parliament expresses itself by a majority of the votes cast. In the overall context, the European Parliament disposes not only of co-legislative but of co-budgetary powers as well.

On the other hand, there are a number of policy domains where the Commission's role is more limited and where decisions require unanimity in the Council. Essentially these domains concern politically sensitive areas such as criminal law and police cooperation, as well as foreign and security policy. In some other domains, the Union has no competence to issue measures aiming at harmonisation of national rules and regulations. The domains of education, culture and public health are examples here.

The Court of Justice, having its seat in Luxembourg, has been conferred upon jurisdiction to control the legality of the acts of the institutions and to safeguard the uniform application and interpretation of EU law provisions. The European Central Bank, having its seat in

Frankfurt, conducts the monetary policy of the Union, together with the national banks of the Member States whose currency is the Euro.[1]

As aforementioned, unity and uniformity are vital principles inherent to the EU cooperation process. Therefore, in principle, EU law and policies apply to all partners in an equal manner. In this way, the stability of the institutional infrastructure and the consistency of the overall EU policies can be ensured.

3 Fundamental values and achievements

The European Union has achieved many positive results. The cooperation started in 1952 and focused at that time on two crucial industrial sectors, coal and steel.[2] On 25 March 1957 – 60 years ago – the EEC Treaty[3] was signed.

Over the decades the Union has become an ever growing area on the European continent where generally speaking human rights are respected and where democracy and the rule of law have been implemented. In that respect the Union's aim to promote peace, its values and the well-being of its peoples[4] has been well served.

A huge achievement concerns the enlargement of the EU, from originally six to now twenty-eight Member States. As to substance, the Union has developed an internal market, a big common economic space replacing the concept of national markets. The internal market, in fact, represents the core business of the EU and refers to an – ever growing – area where goods, persons, capital and services can circulate without internal frontiers.[5] The economic relations within the

---

1 See for the basic institutional rules and principles Title III of the Treaty on European Union (TEU) as well as Part Six, Title I, of the Treaty on the Functioning of the European Union (TFEU).
2 The Treaty establishing the European Coal and Steel Community, entered into for on 23 July 1952.
3 The Treaty establishing the European Economic Community, entered into force on 1 January 1958.
4 See Article 3(1) TEU.
5 See for the definition of the internal market: Article 26(2) TFEU.

internal market are characterised by the application of principles such as non-discrimination and mutual recognition. In order to complement the internal market, policies in the domain of agriculture, transport, environment and climate change have been developed. In an advanced stage of the cooperation a common currency – the Euro – has been introduced. Other areas where the Union is entitled to act, however does not possess exclusive competences, concern asylum and immigration policy as well as foreign policy and defence.[6]

Notably, the enlargement process has spread the fundamental values of peace, stability and prosperity over an ever growing area in Europe. The implementation of the principles of free movement of goods, persons, capital and services has created a framework for intensive cooperation, not only with respect to trade but for example in the areas of research, social policy, education and consumer protection as well.

4 Defects of the EU construction

On the other hand, the EU is suffering from a lack of transparency and, more and more, from a lack of support of the ordinary citizen. Eurosceptical political parties and groups do exist in several Member States and even Eurosceptical governments have emerged.

One of the problems in this regard is that the Union is an abstract construction. It presents itself to the citizen essentially through big office buildings in Brussels, Strasbourg and Luxembourg. The leading personalities and the civil servants working for the institutions (and organs) are hardly visible. For example, the Commission, although it has a crucial role to play as initiator and supervisor of the overall EU cooperation, operates basically behind the façades of office buildings in the European quarter in Brussels. Also, the members of the European Parliament, although being directly elected and conferred upon with important legislative and budgetary tasks, experience difficulties to meet their respective constituencies on a regular basis. The

---

6   See for an enumeration of all policy areas of the EU the list of Part Three of TFEU.

multitude of their activities in political groupings, parliamentary committees and the plenary sessions, plus the fact that they often have to travel, is largely due to this finding.

Furthermore, the division of competences and responsibilities between the Union and its Member States is difficult to assess. In fact, the exact division varies from policy domain to policy domain. There do exist policy domains covered by the so-called *exclusive* EU competences (common commercial policy and monetary policy being examples); policies – in fact by far the majority, at least in number – over which responsibilities are *'shared'* between the Union and the Member States (such as internal market, agriculture, environmental policy, energy and justice and home affairs); and domains where the EU only has been granted so-called *supportive, coordinating* or *supplementing* competences (for example education, culture and the protection and improvement of human health).[7]

Having said that, the EU and its institutions are as visible as the Member States want them to be. Indeed, the Member States are the *'Herren der Verträge'*: they are the contracting parties and they determine the scope of activities of the EU as well as the modalities of the functioning of the institutions. They are also the ones responsible for the implementation, application and enforcement of common rules concluded at the EU level. Hence, the way the EU and its institutions are functioning has been invented to a large extent by the Member States themselves.

Therefore, the Member States also bear the primary responsibility with regard to the non-visibility and non-transparency of the overall EU activities. That said, what may be expected in particular from the members of the Commission and the ones of the European Parliament, is that they give more 'exposure' to their activities in order to gain more confidence from the side of the ordinary citizen.

---

7   See for the categories and areas of Union competences: Part One, Title I (Articles 2 to 6), TFEU.

5 Threats and challenges

These days, the European Union is facing serious threats and challenges both externally and internally. To mention the most important:

With regard to the external threats:
- in the East: the conflict between Russia and Ukraine. The reference obviously is to the Russian annexation of the peninsula Crimea in March 2014 and the unrest in Eastern-Ukraine, the Donbas region;
- in the Middle East: the ongoing civil war in Syria, the unrest in Iraq and the apparent eternal Israel/Palestine conflict;
- in Turkey: the measures restricting the rule of law issued after the failed military coup d'état of 15 July 2016 and the constitutional referendum of 16 April 2017. These developments are the more worrying in view of the fact that Turkey still holds the status of a candidate Member State of the EU;
- in Northern Africa: the lack of political stability, notably in Libya;
- migration: the massive migratory movements originating from Africa, the Middle East and Asia and turning, in the first place, towards the European continent as a safe haven;
- terrorism: the attacks undertaken notably by individuals and groups supported by the militant and terrorist movement of IS (Islamic State) and causing threats and severe casualties in Europe; and, last but not least, although geographically more remote;
- the relationship with the United States: after the coming into office of Donald Trump as it 45th President, concerns are expressed about the support of the United States, at least of its President, for the European integration process as well as for the cooperation in the framework of NATO. The diverging opinions expressed by the new President in that regard create a lot of confusion about the stability of the mutual relationship developed over the centuries with that country.

As to the developments within Europe:
- the economic crisis: dating back to 2008 and having touched upon the national economy and the banking sector in practically all Member States, the crisis is not over yet;

- the migration crisis: in several European countries concerns have been expressed about the impact the crisis has on the national society;
- populism and Euroscepticism: anti-establishment tendencies in a number of Member States have given rise not only to the establishment of Europe critical political movements and parties but equally to the emergence of a number of Eurosceptical governments;
- Brexit: the situation of the United Kingdom, a Member State whose people has voted in favour of a withdrawal from the European Union.[8]

Most substance matters mentioned concern crucial but politically highly sensitive issues. They have in common that they largely concern some of our most fundamental values, namely the stability and security of our European societies. Therefore, the question arises how to counter these problems respectively what the role of the European Union in this process can be.

6 Political sensitiveness and competences

In fact, most problems referred to concern policy matters, for which the responsibility has not been transferred to the European level. What is more, politicians generally speaking are not tempted to hand over their responsibilities in these areas to other instances. The problems touch, as it were, upon the roots of our national societies.

In all areas concerned, the Union certainly has a power to act. However, compared with the scope of the competences of the Member States, the potential involvement of the Union can only be limited and additional in nature.

---

8   As a consequence of the referendum of 23 June 2016. The new Prime Minister Theresa May has notified the EU of the 'intention' of the United Kingdom to leave to Union on 29 March 2017. As from that date the deadline of two years, referred to in paragraph 2 of Article 50 TEU, has started to run.

At the same time, the fact that Member States themselves are still primarily the competent authorities in the domains concerned presents a huge problem. On the one hand, all problems referred to concern issues which individual states are not able to handle (anymore) alone. To that extent all Member States have a clear interest to cooperate intensively in those areas. On the other hand, Member States often are even reluctant to – if only – coordinate their policies regarding the problems mentioned. If at all willing to do so, they easily may differ from opinion how to settle the issues.

7 Voluntariness, a gradual process and heterogeneity
However, there is more:

EU cooperation is a voluntary process. An accession, for example, can only be realised when, first of all, the third state concerned takes the initiative by filing an application thereto. It is only thereafter that negotiations can start to assess whether the minimum requirements for membership are met respectively to establish the conditions and modalities of a possible membership.[9]

EU integration is also a gradual process. Each time, in light of the circumstances and in view of the needs at hand, new goals and targets have to be set. Often the need to undertake complementary action imposes itself. However, we cannot force the Member States to participate in a process setting, from time to time, such new objectives. At any rate, for all these steps a consensus has to be reached.

Moreover, whereas the founding fathers and the first group of acceding Member States represented more or less a homogenous group of like-minded states, the group of present Member States has become more and more heterogeneous. Practice reveals – the reference here is *inter alia* to the tendencies of populism and the series of Eurosceptical governments that have emerged – that not all Member States are prepared anymore to participate in new additional projects at European level.

---

9   See for the whole procedure: Article 49 TEU.

Hence, the environment where we are living in complicates the process to mobilise, each time again, all Member States to simultaneously agree on the next stages of the cooperation process.

8 Existing models of differentiation

For the reasons mentioned above, the question arises whether initiatives for flexible or differentiated cooperation should not be allowed, and even encouraged.

In fact, models of differentiation do exist already in practice. Examples are:

- the Euro cooperation.[10] Only those Member States that fulfil the conditions for the introduction of the Euro – at present 19 – participate. The United Kingdom and Denmark have been formally granted derogations to cooperate in this area. And, although it seems that Sweden does fulfil the necessary conditions, the country does not cooperate either.
- the Schengen cooperation regarding the abolishment of internal border controls respectively the implementation of a common control regime at the external borders of the Union.[11] The United Kingdom and Ireland have been formally granted derogations to cooperate in this domain, whereas Romania, Bulgaria, Cyprus and Croatia do not cooperate as yet.
- the Area of Freedom, Security and Justice cooperation regarding policy domains like visa, asylum and immigration policy as well as criminal law and police cooperation.[12] The United Kingdom and Ireland profit from an 'opt out/opt in' regime. This arrangement allows them to cooperate in this area on an ad hoc basis, to be decided upon by themselves. On the other hand, Denmark does not cooperate at all in this wide domain. For that purpose, that Member State has been granted a full derogation.

---

10 See Article 3(4) TEU, to be read in conjunction with Chapter 2, Title VII TFEU.
11 Originally developed in intergovernmental treaties, at present the subject matter of Article 77 TFEU.
12 See Title V of Part Three TFEU.

- the defence cooperation, in the context of which options have been developed for the benefit of groups of Member States willing to execute certain tasks[13] respectively to establish a permanent structured cooperation.[14]

These examples concern concrete policy areas based on provisions of primary law. What we should aim at, however, is to develop more structural models allowing flexible approaches on an *ad hoc* basis, without having to first amend the treaty texts for that purpose. Such approaches should not necessarily aim at handing over more concrete competences to the EU. They rather intend to create options to facilitate that the treaty objectives, subscribed to by all Member States, can be implemented in practise.

9   Enhanced cooperation

In fact, there already does exist an instrument allowing for cooperation in smaller groups of Member States in order to – as the treaty states – further the objectives of the Union. The reference here is to the principle of enhanced cooperation, the principle introduced by the Amsterdam Treaty.[15]

However, the way enhanced cooperation is organised now, is difficult to apply. It is a remedy of last resort enabling groups of at least 9 Member States to start cooperation once negotiations in the full Council regarding a concrete proposal of the Commission end in an impasse. In such a situation, in order to initiate cooperation in the smaller circle, the Commission has to submit to the Council a specific proposal. On that proposal the Council has to agree by qualified majority whereas the European Parliament has to give its consent. Before enhanced cooperation can be triggered more specifically in the area of common and foreign policy, a request of the Member States

---

13 The so-called 'coalitions of the willing': Articles 42(5) and 44 TEU.
14 Articles 42(6) and 46 TEU.
15 The Amsterdam Treaty entered into force on 1 May 1999.

concerned has to be approved by the Council by unanimity, after having heard the High Representative and the Commission.[16]

Since the principle entered into force in May 1999, the application of enhanced cooperation has been agreed upon in the Council only five times, in rather technical files. Out of these five files, enhanced cooperation has been fully implemented in three of them.[17]

Moreover, as elaborated at present in the treaties, enhanced cooperation in fact provides a wrong and notably too narrow approach. As recalled very small groups – composed of at least 9 Member States – are allowed to start enhanced cooperation. That requirement thus represents only a bit more than one-third of the present number of Member States. Furthermore, acts adopted through enhanced cooperation are not regarded as part of the *acquis* of the Union. Hence on both points a more flexible approach is indicated, justifying the fact that enhanced cooperation is intended to further the objectives of the Union, protect its interests and reinforce its integration process.[18] Therefore, the focus should be on larger, more representative groups, whereas the results of enhanced cooperation should be considered part of the EU *acquis*.

Likewise, the conditions to trigger enhanced cooperation should be simplified. Firstly, the condition concerning a preliminary and specific proposal of the Commission to start enhanced cooperation should be abolished. Indeed, by filing its original proposal the Commission has expressed its interest that action at the level of

---

16 See Article 20 TEU and Articles 326 to 334 TFEU.
17 So far enhanced cooperation has been agreed upon in Council in the following files: Divorce law, the European Unitary patent, Property regimes of international couples, the Financial transaction tax and the European Public Prosecutor. However, the principle has only been implemented in the first three files mentioned: Divorce law, the European Unitary patent and Property regimes of international couples. See https://ec.europa.eu/commission/sites/beta-political/files/enhanced_cooperation_-_already_a_reality_in_the_eu_1.pdf and https://en.wikipedia.org/wiki/Enhanced_cooperation.
18 See the reference in Article 20(1), second sub-paragraph, TEU.

the EU will be taken in the first place. One could argue therefore that, in a situation where a common agreement cannot be reached in the Council, an action taken by a smaller group of Member States is to be considered a 'next best' solution implicitly approved of by the Commission. Also the requirement concerning an explicit approval by the Council should be cancelled.

10 The criterion of three quarters of the number of Member States

Therefore, an idea could be to focus on coalitions of Member States consisting of a clear majority of Member States.

In concrete terms, one may think of groups composed of 'three quarters of the number of Member States'. Out of the presently 28 Member States, that would mean 21 Member States. This number would remain the same even after the possible withdrawal of the United Kingdom from the Union. On the contrary, once more new Member States will have acceded – think for example of the remaining successor states of the former Yugoslavia which are not as yet EU Member States, and Albania – that minimum level might increase up to 22 or 23.

In fact, 'three quarters of the number of Member States' represents a sufficient 'critical mass'. One could, of course, choose other formulas as well, 'four-fifth' or 'five-sixth' or whatsoever. After the example of the arrangements for qualified majority voting,[19] one could also add a second compulsory criterion related to a percentage of the overall population of the European Union. However, the criterion of 'three quarters of the number of Member States' reflects at first sight enough pushing power to have the process moving forward by, as it were, 'forerunners' groups.

---

19   Article 16(4) TEU. See also *infra*, Section 12.

Those Member States not being part of the coalition of three quarters will obviously not be bound by the results of the cooperation in the smaller circle. They, however, can always join later once they are ready and willing to do so.

11 The institutional and legal framework of the EU

Inherent in the proposal just presented is that, once the preliminary condition of three-quarters of the Member States being fulfilled, the group concerned should be able to make use of the institutional and legal framework of the EU. Hence, all institutions and organs would remain involved,[20] like the ordinary set of legal instruments.[21]

The availability of the EU infrastructure indeed is an essential pre-condition. According to the proposed line of thinking, the cooperation will be developed within the structures of the EU and not outside. The idea thus is to build further on the cooperation as developed in the framework of the Union. As a consequence, the scope of the EU cooperation as well as the EU *acquis* will be enlarged accordingly in practice.

12 Or more majority voting?

A question that still may arise is: what is to be preferred, to facilitate structures of flexible cooperation or to introduce more options of (qualified) majority voting in the Council?[22]

In order to advance from the present state of the integration process, the first option (flexibility) is to be preferred over the second one (majority voting). In this respect, it is reminded that the new areas to be entered in all concern sensitive policy domains touching upon

---

20 See for the institutions and the relevant institutional provisions: Title III TEU and Title I of Part Six TFEU.
21 See for the list of legal acts of the Union: Article 288 TFEU.
22 In the treaties 'qualified' majority is defined as at least 55% of the members of the Council comprising at least fifteen of them and representing Member States comprising at least 65 % of the population of the Union: Article 16(3) and (4) TEU.

the roots of national society and identity.[23] Thus, apart from the fact whether the Member States would be prepared to either apply existing possibilities of majority voting in these areas or to create new ones,[24] outvoting of Member States in such sensitive domains will as a rule not help to stabilise and reinforce the EU structures and policies. Equally, the complete and timely implementation of majority decisions cannot be secured.[25]

In short, it is better to facilitate those who want to advance, instead of forcing the non-willing to cooperate.

Having said that, whereas to arrive at a qualified majority in the Council it suffices to mobilise 55% of the members of the Council comprising at least 15 of them, a larger majority should be required to initiate differentiated cooperation. It is for that reason that the earlier presented proposal regarding cooperation of smaller groups of Member States in the framework of enhanced cooperation,[26] refers to the criterion of three-quarters of the number of Member States, so at least 21 instead of 15.

13 A solid basis for EU membership

The intention in all this is certainly not to divide the Union and/or to undermine its structures. On the contrary, stability and peace are – and should remain – the fundamental assets of European integration.

In order to qualify as a 'Member State', first of all, a state has to fulfil the minimum requirements of membership related *inter alia* to respect for human rights, democracy and the rule of law.[27] Such a state

---

23 *Supra*, Sections 2 and 6.
24 In that last case *inter alia* the treaties would have to be amended.
25 The Council decision of 22 September 2015 regarding the relocation of migrants over the Member States is a good example in this context.
26 *Supra*, Sections 9 and 10.
27 See Article 2 TEU.

must participate also in the policy areas covered by the exclusive competences of the European Union.[28]

Besides the state concerned must participate – at least – in the core business of the EU. Such a minimum *acquis* can be presented as follows:
- the internal market cooperation;
- closely related policies such as transport, environmental and climate policy;
- the common asylum and migration policy, so the external dimension of the principle of free movement of persons; and
- the policy making regarding common foreign and security policy (CFSP) and common security and defence policy (CSDP).

The nature of the policy domains listed when viewed collectively guarantees that a solid common framework of cooperation arises, in the context of which all Member States are tied together by uniform procedures ensuring a proper degree of discipline.

On the contrary, beyond the scope of such an *acquis* at minimum level, more flexibility could be allowed without the stability and solidity of the overall infrastructure being put in danger.

14 Enlargement

Such a model could also be offered to third countries that have an interest to become a Member State of the EU. Such countries would have to comply with the minimum requirements for membership of Article 2 TEU just referred to, and to subscribe to all objectives outlined in the existing treaty texts. On the other hand, once the countries concerned would be able to demonstrate that they are able to participate in the cooperation regarding the minimum *acquis* as explained, they should, in principle be entitled to formally accede. Participation in the other domains can then be dealt with later, once they are able and willing to do so.

---

28 Article 3 TFEU where the reference *inter alia* is to customs union, monetary policy and common commercial policy.

Such an approach – opening up the membership of the European Union to an ever-growing number of states – should not be understood as a threat to the quality of the EU cooperation. As long as states admitted as 'Member States' do participate in all dimensions of the described *acquis* at a minimum level, the stability of the organisation and, likewise, the consistency of the policies concerned can be assured.

On the other hand, as a consequence, the values of peace and stability would be spread over an ever growing geographical area.

15 Brexit and the United Kingdom

Can the suggested framework for EU membership help the United Kingdom (UK), the Member State which is now on its way out of the European Union?

In principle, the answer could be in the affirmative. On the other hand, in her speech of 17 January 2017,[29] Prime Minister Theresa May has declared that the UK does not want to participate anymore in the internal market cooperation. Instead, the UK may content itself to conclude a – simple – free trade agreement with the Union. That approach is astonishing in view of the fact that a simple free trade arrangement offers so much less compared to what the internal market cooperation does offer at present.

Moreover, one of the main reasons to withdraw from the EU concerns the impact free movement of workers – from within the Union to the United Kingdom – is assumed to have on the British society, notably the employment situation, its public resources and the business environment in the UK. In a way, that also is a surprising position in light of the deal former Prime Minister Cameron had agreed upon in February 2016 in the European Council.[30]

---

29 www.gov.uk/government/speeches/the-governments-negotiating-objectives-for-exiting-the-eu-pm-speech.
30 The reference is to the Decision of 18/19 February 2016 of the Heads of State or Government, meeting within the European Council, concerning a new Settle-

Indeed, the European Council confirmed at that occasion in the first place that the free movement of workers may be subject to limitations on grounds of public policy, public security or public health. It added then – the reference is to the so-called 'rule of reason' doctrine developed by the Court of Justice on a case by case basis – that free movement of workers may be restricted if overriding reasons of public interest make it necessary, by measures proportionate to the legitimate aim pursued. As specific grounds the European Council – Prime Minister Cameron at that time being one of them – referred to: encouraging recruitment, reducing unemployment, protecting vulnerable workers and averting the risk of seriously undermining the sustainability of social security.[31] On top of that the Commission stated in an accompanying declaration that it would table a proposal to amend Regulation 492/2011 (on freedom of movement of workers within the Union) to provide for a safeguard mechanism. This on the understanding that it can and will be used as a solution to the United Kingdom's concerns about the exceptional inflow of workers from elsewhere in the European Union that is has seen over the years.[32]

Hence, the arrangements of February 2016 in fact offered an adequate framework to keep the functioning of the principle of free movement of workers under control!

Furthermore, the UK intends to organise its asylum and migration policy itself. Now, leaving aside that the UK – as recalled earlier –[33]

---

ment of the United Kingdom within the European Union, doc. EU EUR 1/16 of 19 February 2016.

31   See the Decision of 18/19 February 2016, already cited, Section D. Social Benefits and Free Movement, p. 20.

32   See doc. EU EUR 1/16 of 19 February 2016, p. 34. In an additional paragraph it was said: 'The European Commission considers that the kind of information provided to it by the United Kingdom, in particular as it has not made full use of the transitional periods of free movement of workers which were provided for in recent Accession Acts, shows [that] the type of exceptional situation that the proposed safeguard mechanism is intended to cover exists in the United Kingdom today. Accordingly, the United Kingdom would be justified in triggering the mechanism in the full expectation of obtaining approval.'

33   *Supra*, Section 8.

has been granted an opt-out regarding the Area of Freedom, Security and Justice cooperation as a whole, all areas just referred to – free movement of persons as a dimension of the internal market cooperation, as well as asylum and migration policies – belong as to content to what earlier has been described as a minimum *acquis* of EU membership. Therefore, as long the UK would not be willing to comply with the relevant treaty obligations concerned, that country cannot qualify – in the framework of its 'future relationship' with the Union –[34] as an EU Member State.

16 Unity and uniformity

Certainly we should keep the essentials of EU cooperation, such as unity and uniformity, intact in the future.[35] Each and every Member State is thus – and should remain – entitled to participate in each and every policy domain covered by the EU competences and responsibilities.

In fact, Member States are supposed to do so in view of the fact that they have accepted all treaty objectives upon their accession to the Union. It is only because, as has been explained, simultaneousness and synchronism as regards the implementation of these objectives are difficult to achieve these days that instruments of flexibility are to be welcomed. Or, to put it in more honest terms, in view of the heterogeneity as manifested in the course of time between the Member States with regard to their willingness to follow the path of an ever closer union,[36] time has come to create more flexibility options in order to fully exploit the potential of the integration process and to safeguard the sustainability of that process in future.

---

34 The reference is to the wording of Article 50(2) TEU.
35 See for the importance of such principles *supra*, Sections 1 and 2.
36 See the wording of Article 1 TEU.

17 White Paper Commission

In the meantime Commission President Juncker submitted on
1 March 2017 his White Paper of the Future of Europe.[37] In his paper,
Juncker presents reflections and scenarios for the European Union
of 27 Member States by 2025.[38]

More particularly the Commission proposes five scenarios:
- Carrying on
- Nothing but the single market
- Those who want to do more
- Doing less more efficiently
- Doing much more together

As regards the follow-up of his White Paper, Juncker proposed a broad
debate to start across Europe. Juncker will give his personal views
on the ideas submitted in his White Paper, in his 'State of the Union'
speech before the European Parliament in September 2017. Thereafter
the European Council is supposed to draw some first conclusions by
the end of 2017. It is then up to that same European Council to decide
on the course of action to be rolled out in time for the European Parliament elections in June 2019. Apparently, Juncker is of the opinion
that by that time – mid 2019 – final conclusions regarding the future
of EU cooperation may be drawn.

Certainly it is to be welcomed that the discussion about the future of
the European integration process has been initiated at the (highest)
political level. In fact, that had become high time. In this respect,
reference has to be made only to the serious threats and challenges
the European Union is faced with these days.[39]

---

37 https://ec.europa.eu/commission/sites/beta-political/files/white_paper_on_the_
future_of_europe_en.pdf. See also Press release: opa.eu/rapid/press-release_IP-
17-385_en.htm.
38 Apparently the Commission President assumes that by that time – 2025 – not
only the United Kingdom has left the EU, but also that no new Member States
will have acceded.
39 *Supra*, Section 5. In practise, it was only after the British referendum of 23 June
2016 that the leaders of the remaining 27 Member States started consultations

On the other hand, the scenarios proposed are rather disappointing. In fact, Juncker proposes five options, whereas according to his own way of thinking in fact many more could be thought of. Other comments can also be made:

Scenario 1: Carrying on
This scenario implies that life continues working with the instruments and procedures available at present. In short, the reference is to 'muddling through'. That, however, is clearly not a solution. Practice shows this on a daily basis. On the contrary, choices have to be made such as whether we want more or less Europe. And, if a preference is manifested in favour of more Europe, the question follows on how to organise the exercise of such additional responsibilities for the Union.

Scenario 2: Nothing but the single market
This scenario is hardly ambitious. In fact, it shows the way to a future based on (much) less substance of cooperation compared to what has been achieved today.

Scenario 3: Those who want to do more
The reference here is to a multi-speed Europe, enabling those Member States who want to proceed to do so in smaller groups. Such a result indeed resembles the proposals put forward in the present publication. However, whereas the Commission scenario refers to specific policy domains, the proposals introduced in this publication promote a more global approach enabling Member States to choose targets and objectives that are deemed necessary in given political circumstances.[40]

---

about the future of the EU cooperation. A first result was the so-called Bratislava Declaration and Roadmap of 16 September 2016, which set out the objectives of work for the coming months: www.consilium.europa.eu/en/meetings/european-council/2016/09/16-informal-meeting/. A second step is reflected by the so-called Rome Declaration of the leaders of 27 Member States and of the European Council, the European Parliament and the European Commission of 25 March 2017, issued at the occasion of the celebration of 60 years after the signature of the EEC Treaty: www.consilium.europa.eu/press-releases-pdf/2017/3/47244656633_en.pdf.

40   *Supra*, Sections 9, 10 and 12.

Scenario 4: Doing less more efficiently
Certainly, 'efficiency' should be always welcomed. However, focusing on less targets and objectives compared to the situation as it is today demonstrates a model of low ambition.

Scenario 5: Doing much more together
This model certainly looks interesting. However, in view of the fact that this option includes consensus as the point of departure for the decision making in the future stages of EU cooperation, the model does not seem very realistic.

All in all, Juncker's proposals focus on a selection of specific policy matters. To that extent, the proposals of the White Paper are rather static. For example, when choosing for the one or the other scenario, the question arises how to deal with more general and global issues such as 'security'. Because, essentially all threats and challenges the Union is confronted with these days, whether they concern geopolitical threats, migration or terrorism, are related to security, one way or the other.

On the contrary, the inherent characteristic of the proposals presented in the present publication is that EU cooperation is a gradual process, characterised by a 'step by step' approach. Therefore, the idea is that we rather need a flexible but structural model which can be applied when considered necessary in the circumstances at hand. In short, there needs to be an adequate procedure to manage 'the process'. In doing so, the focus is on a majority of three quarters of the number of Member State taking the lead in the further stages of EU cooperation, whereas the other Member States can follow once they are willing and prepared to do so. At any rate, EU cooperation is open for all.

18 Treaty amendment procedure
A further proposal, however closely connected to the earlier ones, is that we should practice the criterion of three quarters of the number of Member States also with regard to the procedure for treaty amendments.

At present consensus is required for all successive stages of the negotiations to amend the treaties: the agreement reflecting the results of the negotiations; the signature of the amending treaty texts; the approval of the treaty amendments at the national level; and their entry into force.[41] Instead, and that is what now is proposed, it should suffice that once three-quarters of the number of Member States is willing to subscribe to new objectives and targets, such a majority is entitled to amend the treaty texts for that purpose.

Currently, at the present state of EU law, two variants of a so-called simplified revision procedure do exist, both of them introduced by the Lisbon Treaty:
- Amendment of all or part of the provisions of Part Three TFEU relating to the internal policies and action of the Union.[42] According to this procedure, it is up to the European Council to take a unanimous decision, after having consulted the European Parliament and the Commission;[43]
- Amendment of the modalities of decision making in a given area: from unanimity to qualified majority voting, and from the application of the 'special' legislative procedure to the 'ordinary' one.[44] According to this – second – procedure, the European Council can act by unanimity after having obtained the consent of the European Parliament.

However, whereas these options for sure represent progress, they are in all honesty to be qualified as treaty amendments of a relatively low importance. For example, the application of both procedures still requires a formal approval by all Member States before the amendments concerned can enter into force.[45]

---

41 Article 48(2-5) TEU.
42 Article 48(6) TEU.
43 Also the European Central Bank has to be consulted in case of institutional changes in the monetary area: Article 48(6), second sub-paragraph, TEU.
44 Article 48(7) TEU.
45 In case of amendments to Part III TFEU, the first option, an approval by all Member States has to be provided in accordance with their respective constitutional requirements, which in practice refers to approval by national parliaments

Therefore, and in order to bring Union cooperation really forward, a more far-reaching formula has to be considered. That is why it is proposed to practise the criterion of three-quarters of the number of Member States also with regard to the 'ordinary' revision procedure, more particularly in the stages regarding the negotiations about proposed treaty amendments, the signature of the results of those negotiations as well as the approval thereof at the national level.

In a way, such proposals bear resemblance with the procedures laid down in the general rules of the Vienna Convention on the Law of Treaties, concluded at Vienna on 23 May 1969.[46] For example, Article 40 of that convention is based on the hypothesis that not all contracting parties necessarily have to participate in the negotiations to amend a multilateral treaty to which they are bound.[47] Furthermore Article 41 opens the possibility for modification of multilateral treaties (only) between certain of the parties.[48]

Now, as recalled earlier,[49] the EU legal order is unique to the extent that it is characterised by principles such as unity and uniformity. On the other hand, the options of the Vienna Treaty demonstrate that,

---

Article 48(6), second sub-paragraph, TEU. Once applying the second option, related to institutional rearrangements, the amending decision has to be notified to national parliaments. In case (only) one national parliament makes known its opposition, the decision concerned cannot be adopted: Article 48(7), third sub-paragraph, TEU.

46   https://treaties.un.org/doc/Publication/UNTS/Volume%201155/volume-1155-I-18232-English.pdf.

47   Every state entitled to become a party to the treaty shall be entitled to become a party to the treaty as amended, it is said: par. 3. On the other hand, the amending agreement does not bind any state already party to the treaty which does not become a party to the amending agreement: par. 4.

48   According to this provision two or more of the parties to a multilateral treaty may conclude an agreement to modify the treaty as between themselves (alone) if: (a) the possibility of such a modification is provided for by the treaty; or (b) the modification in question is not prohibited by the treaty and: (i) does not affect the enjoyment by the other parties of their rights under the treaty or the performance of their obligations; respectively (ii) does not relate to a provision, derogation from which is incompatible with the effective execution of the object and purpose of the treaty as a whole.

49   *Supra*, Sections 1, 2 and 16.

once many states are legally bound to each other by a multilateral treaty, it is not feasible to expect that all of them will – or are able to – participate in all subsequent amending stages of that treaty.[50]

In all this, of course, the Member State whose national parliament has objected to the amendments adopted by the said majority of three quarters of Member States, shall not be bound thereby. On the other hand, such a Member State can always subscribe to the new treaty texts later.

Moreover, the contents of the amendments adopted by three quarters majority through the application of the simplified ordinary revision procedure should be regarded as a part of the European Union *acquis*, so the same *acquis* as has to be negotiated with candidate Member States. That said, new Member States should not be obliged to respect such new obligations already at the outset of their membership. Like the present Member States not participating, they can 'opt in' once they are prepared and willing to do so.

An important consequence of the new scenario obviously is that individual Member States no longer possess a right to veto new developments, as the situation is now. On the other hand, because a non-willing Member State shall not be bound to such new reforms, it may be concluded that this new approach is legitimate and democratically justified.

---

50 In a study of the Spinelli Group called 'A Fundamental Law of the European Union', 2013 Verlag Bertelsmann Stiftung, Gütersloh, ISBN 978-3-86793-537-1, the possibility of amending the treaties without all Member States agreeing to it has also been dealt with. According to their proposal, no Member State is entitled to block a treaty amendment, whereas for the adoption of such an amendment a majority of three quarters of the Member States is required. According to the same proposal, a treaty amendment 'shall enter into force throughout the Union' either after being ratified by four fifths of the number of Member States representing a majority of the population of the Union, or after having obtained a majority in a referendum held at the same time in all Member States: pp. 85 and 89-91. Now, unlike the proposals put forward in the present publication, the Spinelli option allows for outvoting one or more Member States. Such an outcome, however, is difficult to accept in the context of primary law amendments.

19 An EU Security Council?

Another proposal in the framework of differentiated cooperation concerns the creation of an EU Security Council.[51] This suggestion is related to the status of the European Union, or rather its non-status, as a global actor.

Indeed, one of the main defects of the EU at this moment in time concerns its weakness to act – and be accepted – as an authority in international affairs. Whether the reference is to the conflict between Russia and Ukraine, the eternal problems in the Middle East (Israel and Palestine), the cruel civil war in Syria, the disorder and turmoil in Libya and – since quite some time already – the authoritarian developments in Turkey, Europe hardly presents itself as a credible and firm partner. Since Donald Trump has become President of the US the need for more European 'unity' and, in that context, an adequate common foreign policy has only become more apparent. The same is true for Europe's responsibility, also financially, in defence matters, notably within the NATO framework.

Thus a concrete and real threat is that Europe will be marginalised more and more in the international arena. For an area guaranteeing peace and stability to over 500 million people and representing the second largest economy at world level, this clearly is an unacceptable perspective.

The Union certainly should be able to exercise military pressure. On the other hand, the Union should not have to present itself as a military power on the world scene. Equally, the EU is not expected to

---

51 An idea periodically launched in the past, however never seriously discussed. Most recently France, Germany and Poland called for a European Security Council in a Joint declaration of their Ministers of Foreign Affairs on 28 August2016: www.auswaertiges-amt.de/EN/Infoservice/Presse/Meldungen/2016/160828_ Gemeinsame_Erklärung_Weimarer_Dreieck.html. See in the literature recently Geor Hintzen, Will Sleeping Beauty Wake up? Proposals for a new Global Strategy, in: Governance and Security Issues of the European Union, Challenges Ahead, Editors Jaap de Zwaan, Martijn Lak, Abiola Makinwa, Piet Willems, Asser Press/Springer 2016, ISBN 978-94-6265-143-2, pp. 291-306, notably pp. 301-302.

intervene militarily in areas of intensive conflict. What is required though is the exercise of more 'hard' power than – purely, as is the situation today – 'soft' power. In case of conflicts in Europe and beyond, the Union should as-it-were have the authority to 'impose' itself as a self-evident interlocutor, mediator and/or arbitrator. Europe should be taken seriously in international discussions and negotiations. In so doing, our mission and vision should be to create conditions of stability and peace everywhere in the world.

Therefore, a fast and effective foreign policy mechanism to secure stability and security in Europe and beyond is needed. It is evident that by making use of the instruments available today, such objectives cannot be achieved. Divergent interests of the Member States; a President of the European Council without a mandate; a High Representative of the Union for Foreign Affairs and Security Policy with a vision but – in this case as well – without a mandate; and unanimity as the requirement for decision making, are ingredients for setbacks.[52]

Equally, in view of the present number of Member States, the creation of a new organ, small but representative as to its composition and capable of managing such a proper common foreign policy, is needed.

An EU Security Council could be such an organ. The obvious example in this context is the Security Council of the United Nations.

Most Member States should accept that they can participate only on a rotation basis in meetings of such a Council aiming to set EU positions in extremely sensitive and urgent foreign policy matters. In that sense, the composition of an EU Security Council could be as follows:
- The President of the European Council as its chairman;
- France, Germany and the United Kingdom[53] as permanent members;

---

52 See for the decision making rules and principles regarding CFSP and CSDP: Title V TEU.
53 The moment the UK withdraws from the Union, the country obviously would have to step down as a member of the Security Council.

- The Troika consisting of the present Presidency of the Council, its predecessor and successor;
- Three other Member States, on a rotation basis;[54]
- The High Representative of the Union for Foreign Affairs and Security Policy; and
- The President of the Commission.

Voting rights are to be exercised only by representatives of Member States. An idea could be that the Security Council decides as a rule by unanimity. However, in case a decision is adopted on the basis of a proposal of the High Representative, a qualified majority vote should suffice.[55]

Such an approach would mean that the three 'permanent' members, as well as the other sitting members of the Security Council, *de facto* possess a veto right only in cases wherein the Council has to decide unanimously anyhow. On the contrary, in case the Council can decide by (qualified) majority, such a veto right does not exist.[56] Another consequence would be that the other non-represented Member States, generally speaking, are bound by the decisions of the Council.

That said, a minority of at least four 'non-represented' Member States should be able to 'block' the implementation of an adopted decision.[57] Such a blocking minority should exercise that prerogative within 24 hours after the decision concerned has been taken. Thereafter a new round of discussions must start, in the Security Council complemented by the objecting Member States, in order to arrive at a

---

54 Here the rotation scheme of the Presidency of the Council can serve as a source of inspiration: Council Decision 2016/1316 of 26 July 2016, OJ EU L 208/42 of 2 August 2016.

55 This idea in a way is inspired by the principle of Article 31(2), second indent, TEU.

56 This clearly is a different approach compared to the situation at present when the Council is entitled to decide by qualified majority: see Article 31(2), in particular the second sub-paragraph, TEU.

57 After the example of the principle of Article 16(4), second sub-paragraph, TEU.

common position within 48 hours.[58] In case such a common decision can then not be reached, the competence to take a final decision 'returns' to the Security Council in its ordinary composition. It is then up to that Council to take the final decision, by qualified majority and on the basis of a further proposal of the High Representative. In the context of that last proposal the – remaining – concerns of the objecting Member States should be taken into account.[59]

20 Preliminary condition: amendment of the treaties

In order to have the several suggestions proposed in the present publication adopted – whether they concern enhanced cooperation, the treaty amendment procedure or the establishment of an EU Security Council – first of all the present treaty texts have to be amended by applying the ordinary revision procedure as it is drafted and structured at present. As stated earlier, that is a complicated process.[60]

These days, though, politicians are extremely reluctant to even initiate such discussions. Basically, because they are afraid that if they can agree on such amendments at all, the new treaty texts may be rejected, either by their national parliaments in the context of the approval procedure, or by their citizens once they will be called to express their opinion in a referendum.

Fear and panic, however, are bad motives to base an opinion on. Such an attitude rather reflects a denial of responsibilities than that it can help to find solutions for serious problems. Politicians are supposed to 'show' their voters 'the way' instead of trying to find guidance in sentiments and emotions expressed by them. Even more,

---

58 As a precedent for acting at very short notice, reference can be made to Article 30(2) TEU where it is said that, in cases requiring a rapid decision, the High Representative, of its own motion, or at the request of a Member State, shall convene an extraordinary Council meeting within 48 hours or, in an emergency, within a shorter period.
59 These decision making modalities in a way are inspired by the arrangements of Article 31(2) TEU, second sub-paragraph.
60 Supra, Section 18.

such an approach of reluctance and denial may, in the end, undermine the solidity and sustainability of the overall EU construction.

In this context, it should be recalled that EU integration is a gradual process. Step by step progress has been made. That is why from time to time new goals and targets have to be set. It is inherent to such a process that periodically amendments to the treaties have to be considered, softer and simpler instruments just not being available.

21 Life is getting complicated

Certainly, life at EU level will become complicated once the suggested formulas of differentiated cooperation will be adopted and applied in practice. Such complications can manifest themselves in the functioning of the institutions. The consistency of specific policy domains respectively the overall EU policy generally speaking may be at stake as well.

At the institutional level, a fundamental issue to reflect about concerns the composition of the institutions and the decision-making procedures. However, although the problems should not be underestimated, they must not be exaggerated either. The fact that the overall institutional and legal framework of the Union is made use of when variants of differentiated cooperation will be practised,[61] is basically the main consideration in this discussion.

The *Commission*, for example, represents the general interest of the EU.[62] Therefore, the rule that that institution consists of one national of each Member State,[63] should not be touched upon. For obvious rea-

---

61 *Supra*, Section 11.
62 Article 17(1) TEU.
63 Article 17(4) TEU. Paragraph 5 of that same provision states that the Commission as from 1 November 2014 shall consist of a number of members corresponding to two thirds of the number of Member States. However, the European Council, in light of the concerns of the Irish people on the Treaty of Lisbon, decided on 11 and 12 December 2008 that the Commission shall continue to include one national of each Member State: doc. 17271/08 of the Council of the European Union, p. 3.

sons also the principle that the Commission decides by majority of his members[64] should not be amended.

Similar arguments are valid with regard to the composition of the *Court of Justice*. Indeed, the Court has been entrusted with a global EU-wide task, which is to look after the correct application and interpretation of EU law provisions.[65] In that sense it is logical that, in case differentiated cooperation will be practised, the Court still can consist of one judge from each Member State.[66]

As to the *European Parliament*, the discussion regarding a differentiated composition has already started. Voices have been heard pleading in favour of a smaller composition of the European Parliament serving in the framework of the Euro-cooperation and, for that reason, composed only of members of Euro-countries. However, all Member States have subscribed to all treaty objectives including the ones related to the Euro cooperation. That is the current situation, and will remain the same once more options for differentiated cooperation will have been created and formalised. Moreover, members of the European Parliament (MEP's), strictly speaking, do not represent their Member State but rather its citizens. Hence it may be argued that the Parliament in its normal composition – reflecting the representation of all Member States – must be enabled to fulfil its global mission with regard to all treaty objectives, whether the topic under discussion concerns collective cooperation involving all Member States or differentiated cooperation such as the Euro-cooperation.

With regard to the functioning of the *Council*, the content of binding decisions should not be influenced by the representatives of the Member States not participating in the policy domain concerned. That said, suitable solutions for this problem are already available, namely the ones elaborated in the framework of enhanced cooperation. According to these arrangements, all members of the Council

---

64 Article 250, first sub-paragraph, TFEU.
65 Article 19(1) TEU.
66 Article 19(2), first sub-paragraph, TEU.

may participate in its deliberations, whereas only members of the Council representing the Member States participating in enhanced cooperation, take part in the vote.[67]

As to the substance matter covered by instruments of differentiated cooperation, we should mind that its content does not disrupt the stability and consistency of the *acquis* applicable to all Member States. In other words, differentiated cooperation instruments should not negatively interfere with the functioning of measures which are binding for all Member States. Here, certainly, a careful manoeuvring is required in practice, by all institutions but in particular by the Commission in view of its prerogative to initiate the overall EU cooperation and its responsibility as caretaker of the general EU interest. The preconditions for the application of enhanced cooperation can serve as a source of inspiration in this respect. Enhanced cooperation namely is supposed to not undermine the functioning of the internal market or economic, social and territorial cohesion.[68]

On the other hand, problems are there to be solved. So, it may be that the overall management of the EU cooperation will become more complicated in future, in case more models of differentiation will be applied. However, we must realise that the international environment where we are living in, has become extremely complicated as well. On the contrary, the present EU instruments available to cope with these problems are not flexible and effective enough to ensure timely and adequate responses.

---

67 Article 330 TFEU. Unanimity shall be constituted by the votes of the representatives of the participating Member States only. For the definition of qualified majority Article 330 TFEU refers to Article 238(3) TFEU. In that provision a qualified majority is defined – under a. – as at least 55 % of the members of the Council representing the participating Member States and comprising at least 65 % of the population of these states, whereas a blocking minority must include at least the minimum number of Council members representing more than 35 % of the population of the participating Member States, plus one member, failing which the qualified majority shall be deemed to be attained.
68 Article 326 TFEU.

22 And, what about the citizen?

The support of the citizen for the European integration process is a huge problem these days. Nobody can deny that. Questions are raised about the usefulness and the added value of membership of the European Union. Equally, people ask themselves why at all it is that we are involved in a process of cooperation at the European level. What was – and what still is – the narrative?

EU cooperation has been initiated and further developed after the Word Wars to secure peace and stability on our continent. These objectives have essentially been achieved. As recalled earlier, we have celebrated on 25 March 2017 the signature of the EEC Treaty, basically the founding treaty of European integration, exactly 60 years ago. Still the greatest part of our continent – and, at any rate, the whole territory of the European Union – can profit from the presence of such fundamental values. Sometimes one gets the impression that people have forgotten about the origin and the causes of cooperation at European level.

Be that as it may, as discussed the Member States and the EU as a whole are confronted these days with a number of global threats and challenges, externally as well as internally, which we cannot handle on our own. We, therefore, have to join forces. We must act together.

To win the support of the citizen for the process of EU cooperation is to a large extent a matter of proper communication and of accountability. The story has to be explained, *i.e.* the whole story and not only selected elements.

To develop such an adequate communication system is primarily the responsibility of *national politicians*, in the first instance the ministers: they represent their Member States in the Brussels arena; they are the best placed to provide explanations about what actually happened in the conference room; and they are the obvious personalities to be held accountable for the results of the negotiations.

To communicate well is naturally an obligation of the *EU institutions* as well. In particular, the members of the European Parliament are supposed to be visible and accessible for their voters. However, because of their meetings and other commitments in Brussels and Strasbourg as well as their regular travel obligations, only little time is left to visit their home regions. As mentioned earlier, the nature of the role of the Commission as initiator and supervisor of the EU cooperation does not enable the members of the Commission to present themselves regularly to the public. In fact, generally speaking, the institutional setup of EU cooperation is such that members and activities of the institutions and organs are hardly visible in practice. That is a serious problem, first of all, for the institutions themselves. That said, the solution to resolve at least a part of this communication problem is left to their members, notably Commissioners and members of the European Parliament.[69]

Then *education*: obviously, schools and universities have a responsibility to inform and instruct their students about 'Europe', its history and culture, topical issues and the future perspectives of the EU cooperation. In fact, we cannot start such a debate early enough. By the way, probably, when lecturing for example 'history' or 'social studies' at the primary or secondary school level, it would be better to start talking with pupils about what happens today in Europe, in the present, and from there on to 'move back' to the past.

At the same time, there needs to be a commitment from the *media*. The media and journalists possess all the means to inform the public at large about relevant developments, at the national and the international level, hence at the European level as well.

Last but not least, we need a commitment of the *citizens* themselves. They are used to listen to the radio, to watch TV and to play computer games, often several hours per day. Can we not expect them to also take an interest, from time to time, in what happens beyond our

---

69   See for this discussion also *supra*, Section 4.

geographical borders? With the help of today's communication facilities, such as the internet and social media, information about the EU and her activities is more accessible.

The question may still arise whether to have to communicate about EU affairs is more difficult – for politicians, civil servants and journalists – than it is to communicate about national affairs. That is highly questionable. Basically it is rather about the willingness to make real efforts. By the way, are politicians so successful in their communication about national issues? And, is the ordinary citizen really aware and interested in what happens at the national level, for example in national parliaments? One may have doubts here.

So, it seems that at both levels – the national and the international, and thus also the European, level – the communication about politics has to be improved substantially.

For the aforementioned reasons, let us not underestimate but not overestimate the communication problems with the ordinary citizen either. We should be able to solve those problems if at least all stakeholders involved are committed to doing that.

At any rate, adequate and complete information and communication about the EU cooperation is the best remedy to obtain the support of the citizens.

23 Final remarks
'Stability' and 'security' for the people, that is essentially what we have to achieve these days, in Europe and beyond.

'United in diversity' was the motto of the Union as enshrined in the European Constitution.[70] The motto thus reflected flexibility. In fact,

---

70 Article I-8: The symbols of the Union: https://europa.eu/european-union/sites/ europaeu/files/docs/body/treaty_establishing_a_constitution_for_europe_ en.pdf.

both concepts – unity and diversity – refer to the way cooperation is organised at EU level.

The same is true for 'stability' and 'differentiation'. Indeed, both concepts are not contradictions or antipodes. They can be applied simultaneously and function in parallel, hand in hand.

So, applying models of differentiated cooperation does not undermine the stability of the overall EU construction, whether it concerns the content of the common policies or the functioning of its institutions. As long as all Member States participate in the cooperation regarding a solid substantive *acquis* at a minimum level, there should be no fear for the emergence of divergence.

Apart from that, the time has come to acknowledge that it is better to facilitate those Member States who want to make progress and deepen their cooperation, instead of forcing the non-willing Member States to participate in that process.

The conclusion, therefore, is that differentiation is a remedy to allow the European Union to advance, to make progress and to survive in future, in the interest of all interested parties: the citizens, the Member States and the Union itself.

Selected bibliography

De toekomst van de Europese Unie-samenwerking, Op zoek naar een hervormd en duurzaam samenwerkingsmodel waaraan ook niet-Europese landen kunnen meedoen, SEW Tijdschrift voor Europees en economisch recht, Uitgeverij Paris, 60e Jaargang, nr. 11 van november 2012, pp. 438-450.

Europa en de Burger, Hoe verder met de Europese Unie-samenwerking? Intreerede De Haagse Hogeschool 24 januari 2013, 56 pagina's, ISBN 978-90-73077-48-5.

The New Institutional Balance of Power in the European Union, in: Which Way Forward, Present Challenges, Strategic Choices and Future Perspectives of the EU, Theseus publication, Fritz Thyssen Stiftung, September 2013, ISBN 978-3-487-14831-1, pp. 32-38.

De voortgang van de Europese Integratie, Wisselwerking tussen recht en beleid ('Progress of the European integration process, Interaction between Law and Policy'), valedictory lecture of 14 March 2014 at the Erasmus University Rotterdam, Erasmus Law lectures 35, Boom Juridische uitgevers 2014, ISBN 978-90-8974-996-3.

De Europese Unie-samenwerking: hoe leggen we het uit?, in: Europese Verkiezingen, Heel belangrijk, Editors Jaap de Zwaan en Chris Aalberts, De Haagse Hogeschool, Lectoraat European Integration, mei 2014, pagina's 31-37.

European Integration and Democracy: A gradual process, with certain limits, contribution to the European Group of Public Law (EGPL) Conference of 13-14 September 2014 in Spetses, Greece, dedicated to 'New Challenges of Democracy/Nouveaux défis à la démocratie' and organised by the European Public Law Organisation (EPLO) in Athens, Greece, European Public Law Series/Bibliothèque de droit public européen, Volume CXVI, EPLO 2015, ISBN 978-618-81949-1-5, pages 219-266.

Flexibility, Differentiation and Simplification in the European Union: Remedies for the Future?, in: Governance and Security Issues of the European Union, Challenges ahead, Editors Jaap de Zwaan, Martijn Lak, Abiola Makinwa, Piet Willems, Asser Press/Springer 2016, ISBN 978-94-6265-143-2, pages 331-353.

The European Union in crisis: is there a need to change its constitutional structures?, contribution to the 6th International Scientific Conference of the Faculty of Law of the University of Latvia, Riga, 16-17 November 2016, published on www.lu.lv/fileadmin/user_upload/lu_portal/apgads/PDF/Book_Juristu_6_konf_II-dalja.pdf, pp. 7-17, as part of a compendium published on the website of the University of Latvia: http://www.lu.lv/apgads/izdevumi/elektroniskie-izdevumi/konferencu-materiali/

About the author

Professor Jaap W. de Zwaan is an emeritus Professor of the Law of the European Union at the Law School of Erasmus University Rotterdam and former Professor European Integration at the The Hague University of Applied Sciences.

He was born in 1949 in Amsterdam, and studied Law at Leiden University and the College of Europe in Bruges, Belgium. In 1993 he obtained his PhD degree in Law at the University of Groningen with a thesis entitled 'The Permanent Representatives Committee, its role in European Union decision making'.

De Zwaan started his professional career in 1973 as a member of the The Hague Bar.

From 1979 until 1998 he worked for the Dutch Ministry of Foreign Affairs in The Hague (European Integration Department and Legal Service) as well as in Brussels (Permanent Representation of the Netherlands at the EU). During his work in The Hague (1979-1983 and 1988-1995) he acted inter alia as Agent for the Netherlands Government in numerous cases before the Court of Justice of the European Union in Luxembourg. As Legal Advisor of the Permanent Representation (1983-1988 and 1995-1998) he was involved in the negotiations on and the drafting of several European treaties, such as the Treaty of Accession of Spain and Portugal to the European Communities, the European Single Act and the Treaty of Amsterdam. In the period 1995-1998 he also was involved in the development of the Justice and Home Affairs cooperation of the European Union.

In 1998 Jaap de Zwaan was appointed full time professor of the Law of the European Union at Erasmus University Rotterdam. In that capacity he was involved in teaching and research with regard to European law and policy. He also participated in several international frameworks of interuniversity cooperation. In the period 1999-2001 he was Dean of International Affairs of his faculty. In the period 2001-2004 he served the Erasmus Law School as Dean.

In September 2005 De Zwaan was appointed Director of the Netherlands Institute of International Relations, 'Clingendael', a think tank as well as diplomatic academy specialized in European studies, international security issues, diplomacy studies and international energy questions.

In May 2011 De Zwaan returned to the Erasmus University Rotterdam. In March 2014 he gave his valedictory lecture at the university.

In May 2012 he was appointed, on a part-time basis, Professor European Integration at the The Hague University of Applied Sciences. On 24 March 2017 he delivered his farewell lecture at that university.